MG KIDS ABC FRUIT AND VEGGIES COLORINGBOOK FOR KIDS AGES 4-8

By Charles Lovjoy

Copyright © 2021 MG KIDS. First Edition. ISBN: 978-1-7359864-5-6

MG KIDS

In Association with

MUSCLE GANG PUBLICATIONS

Poetry by
Charles Lovjoy

Book Cover Design By
Charles Lovjoy, cover image by brgfx/freepik

THIS
BOOK
BELONGS
TO

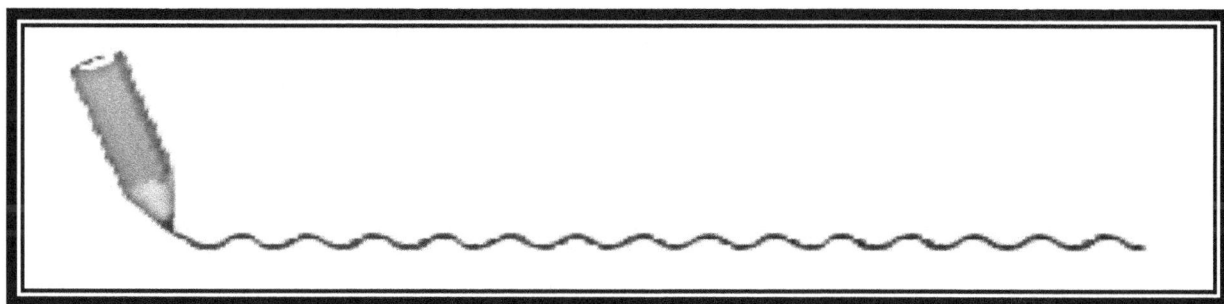

Aa

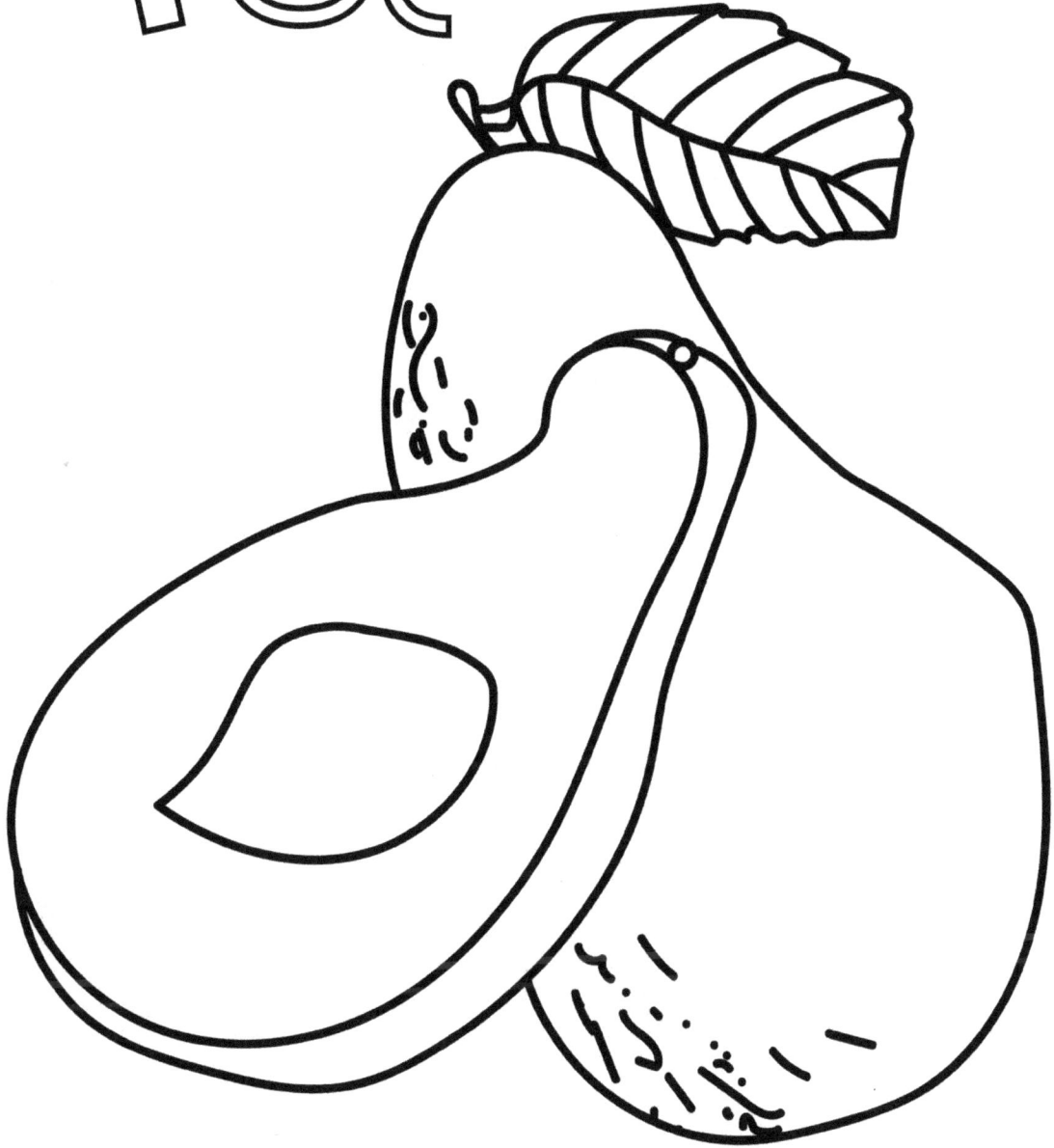

avocado

Bb

broccoli

Cc

carrot

Dd

daikon

Ee

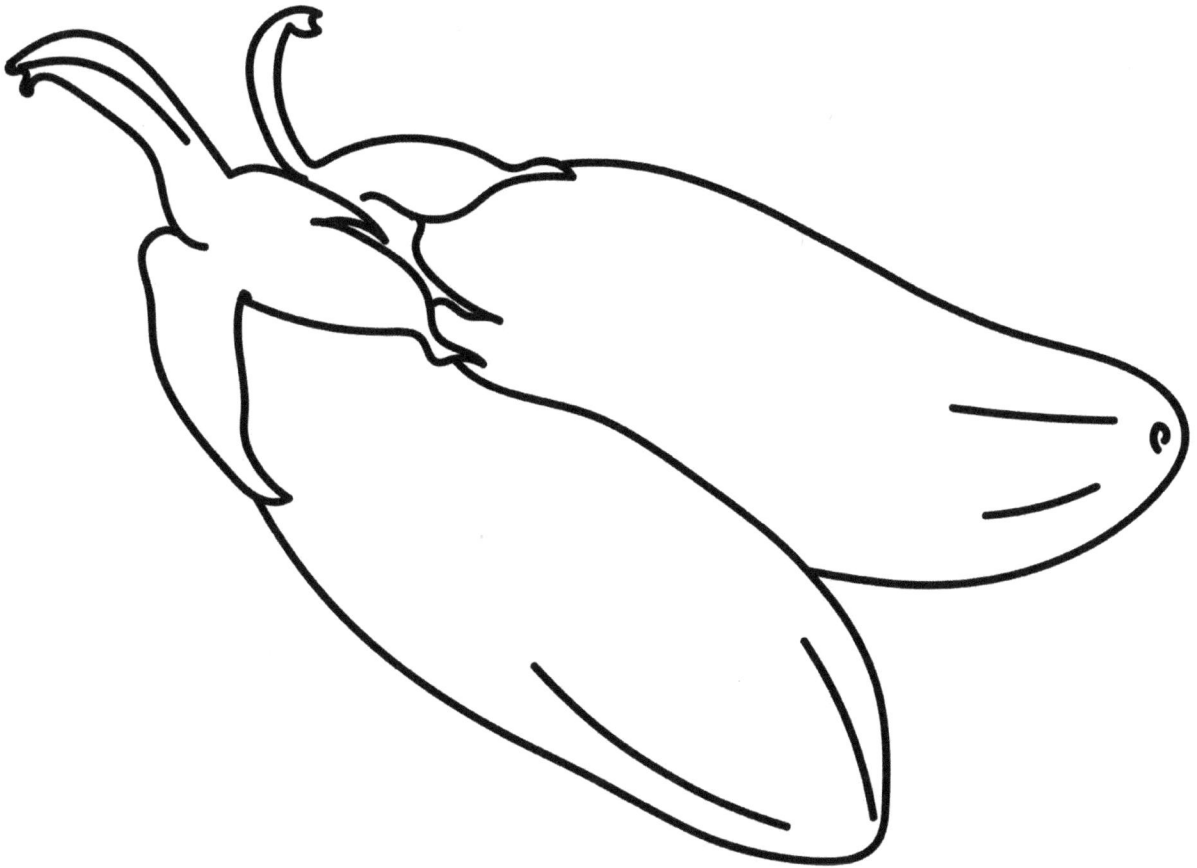

eggplant

F f

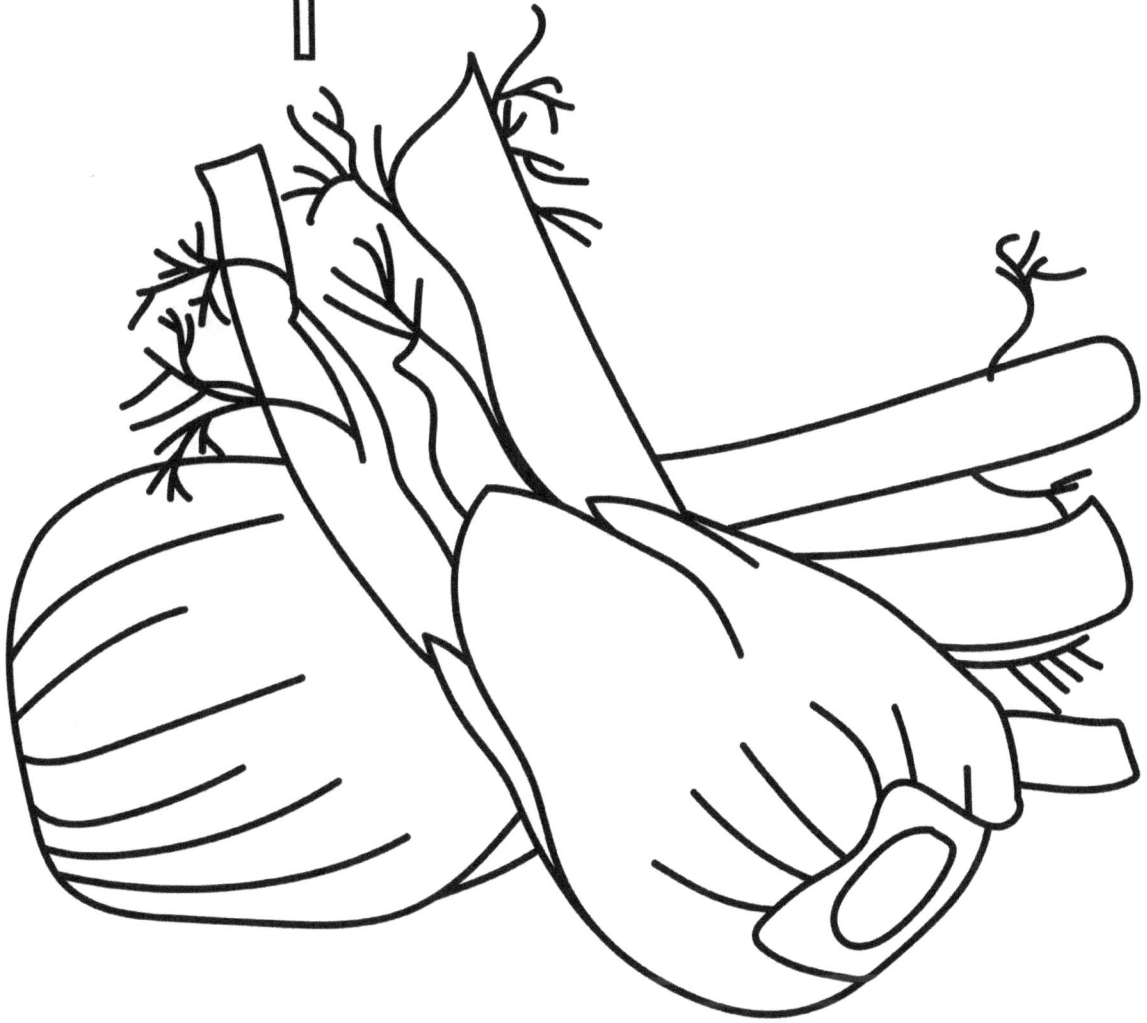

fennel

Gg

garlic

Hh

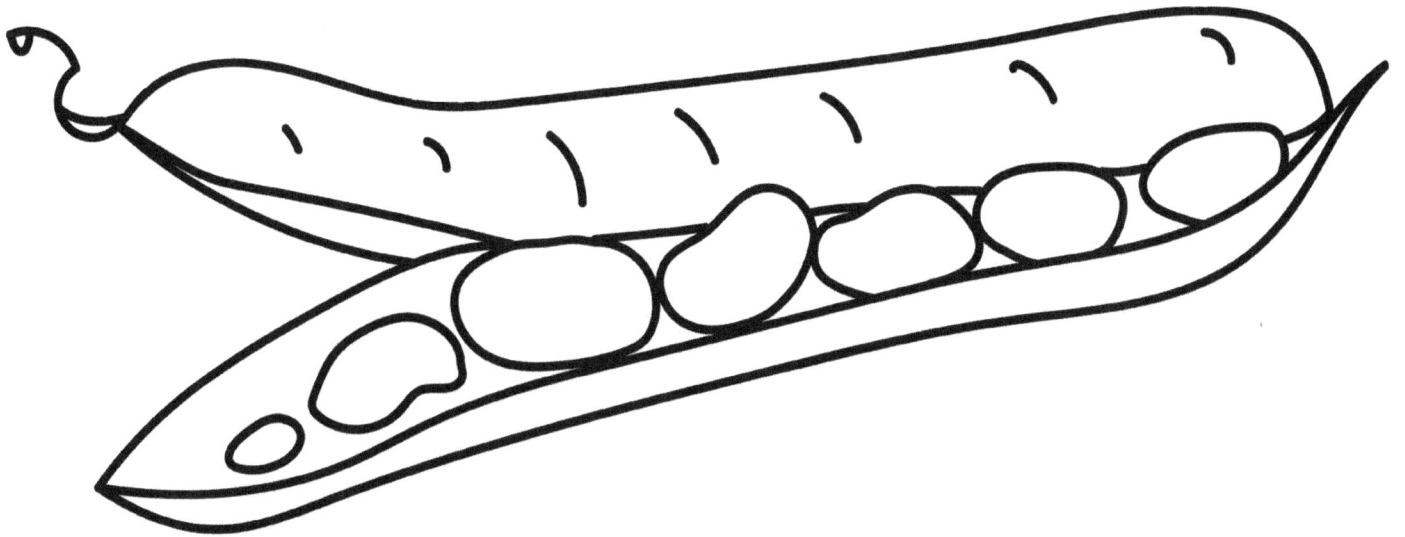

haricot

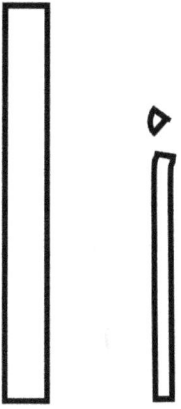

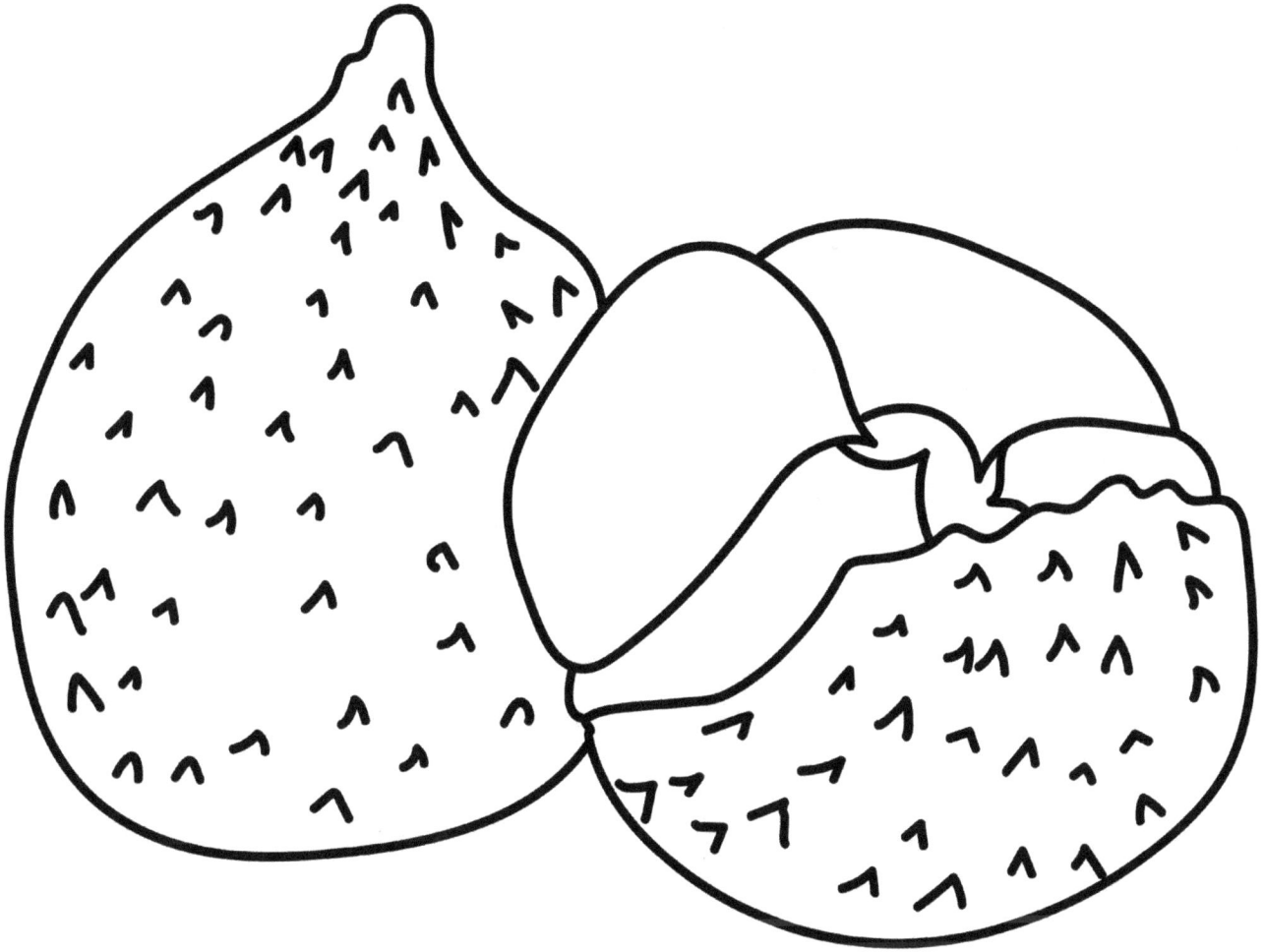

Ii

ita palm

Jj

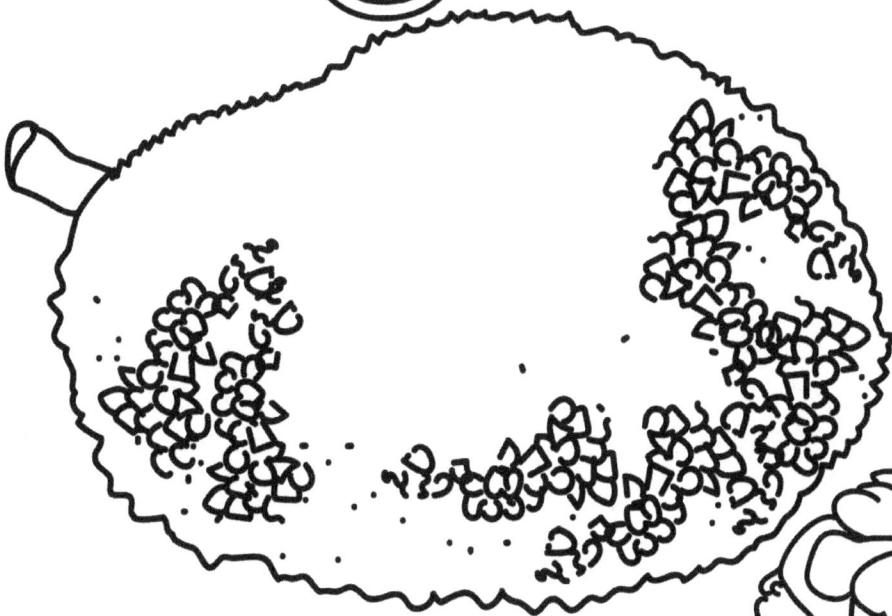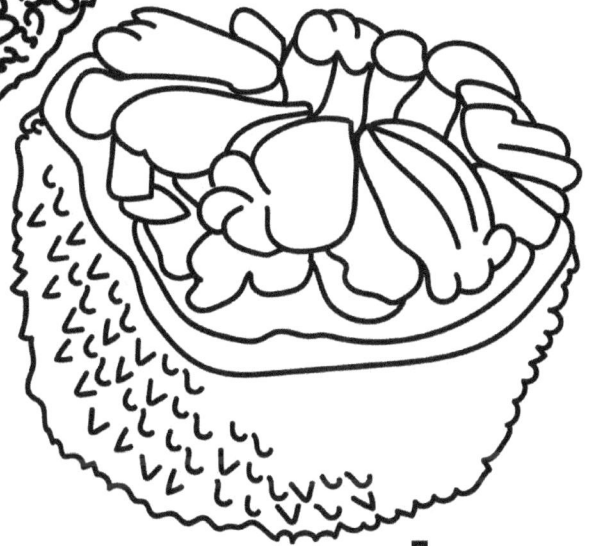

jackfruit

Kk

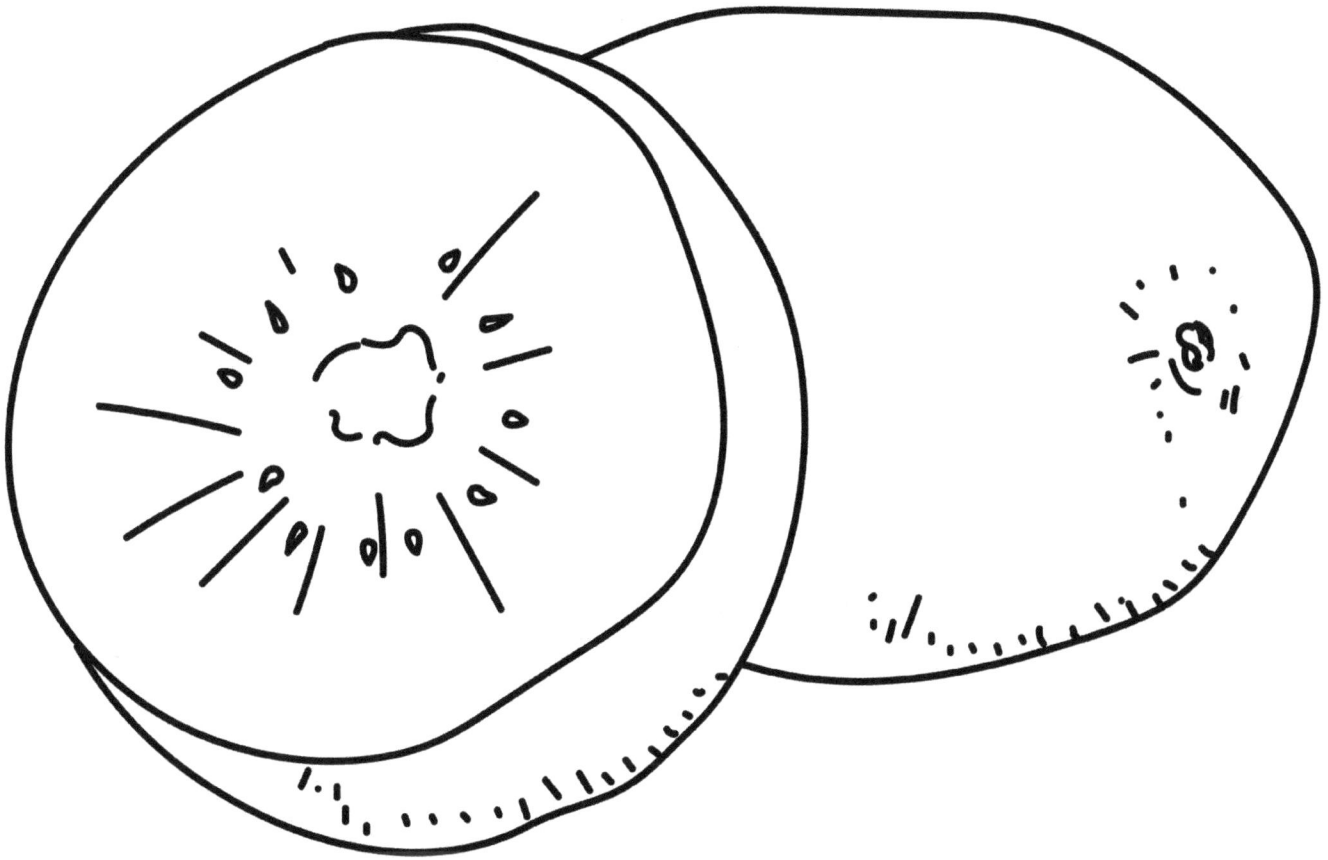

kiwi

Ll

lemon

Mm

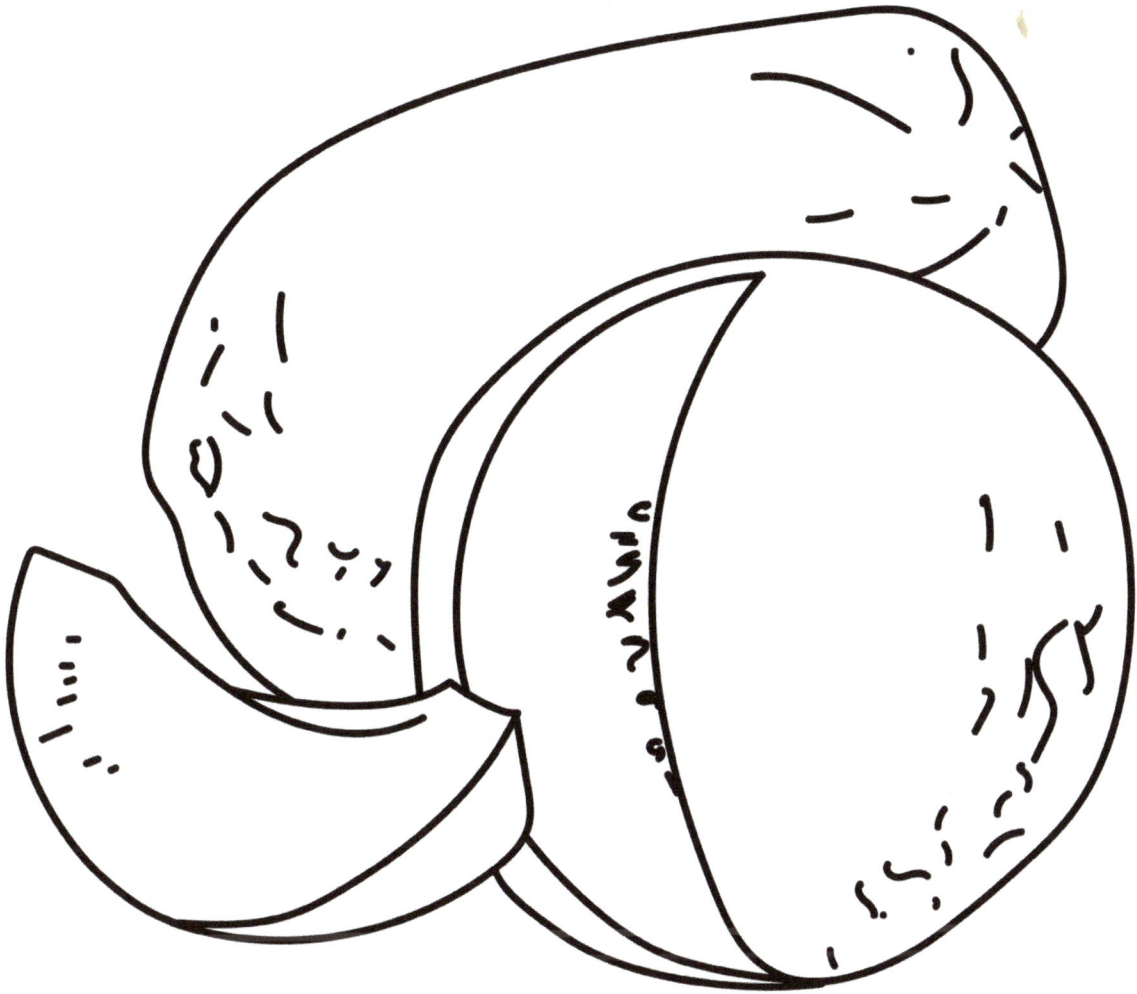

melon

N n

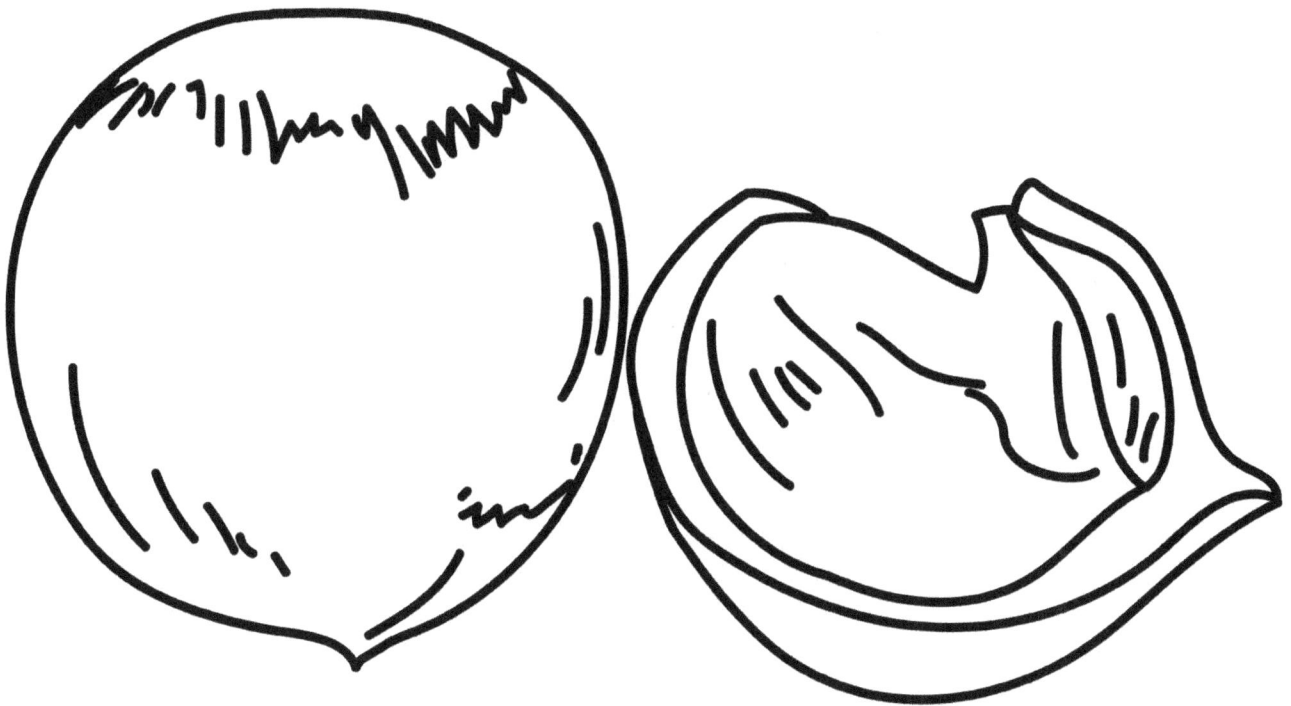

nut

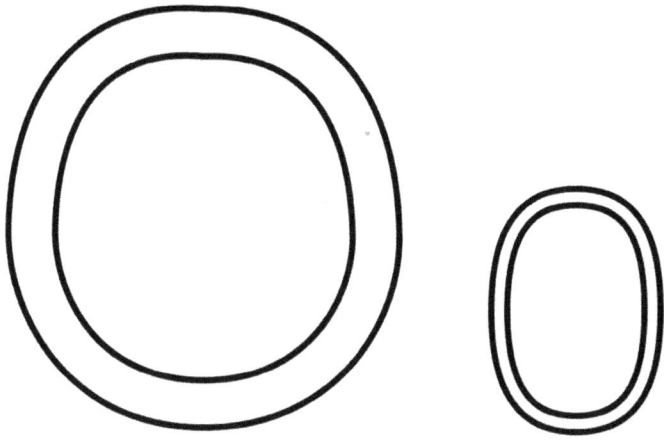

O o

olive

P p

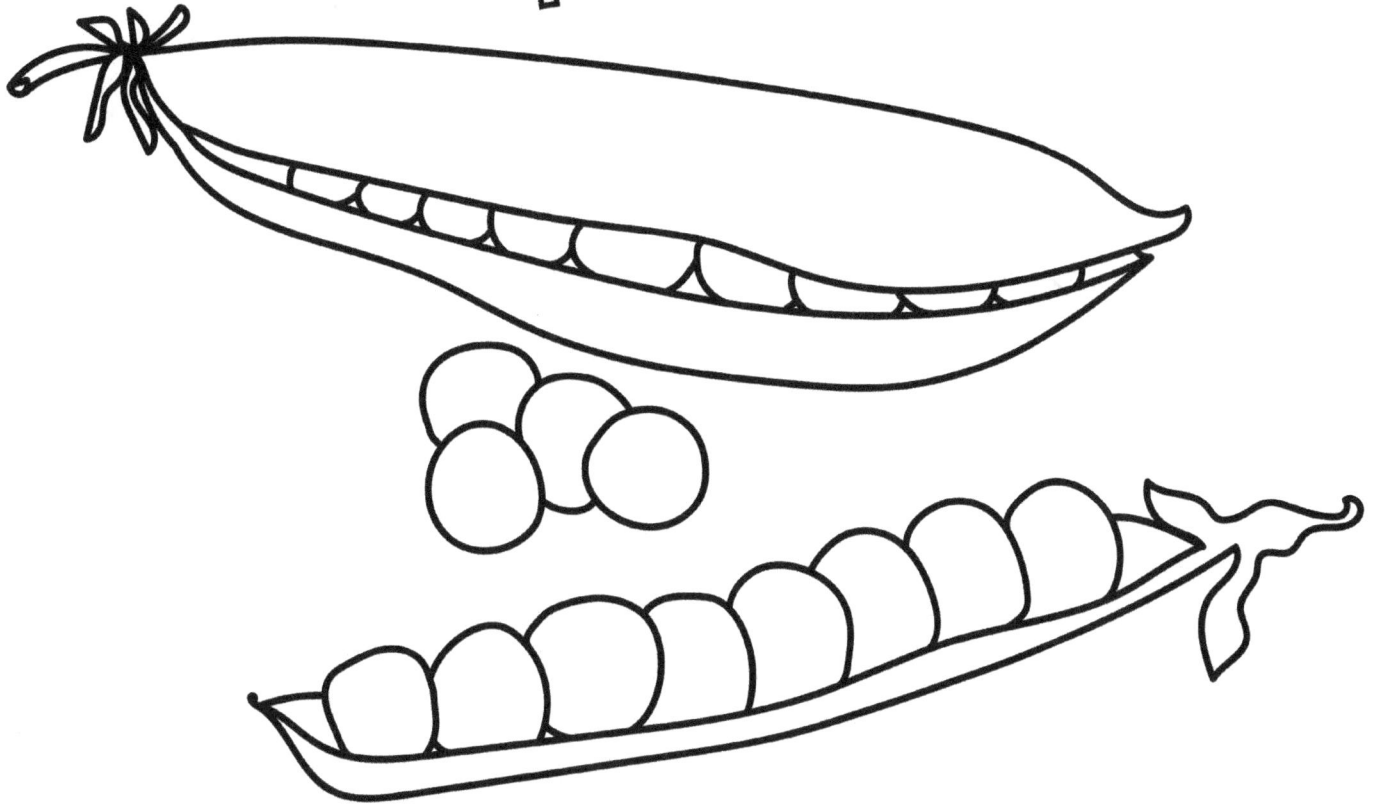

pea

Qq

quince

Rr

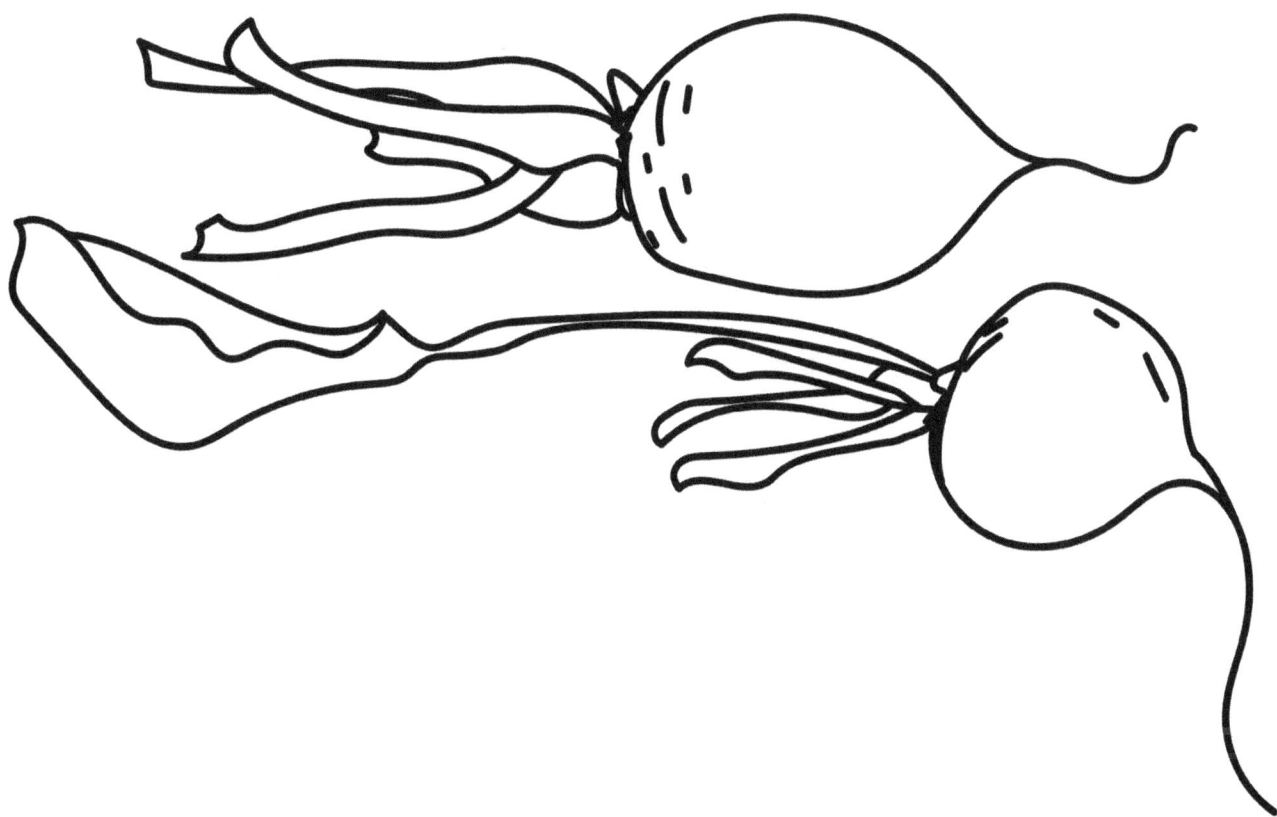

radish

S s

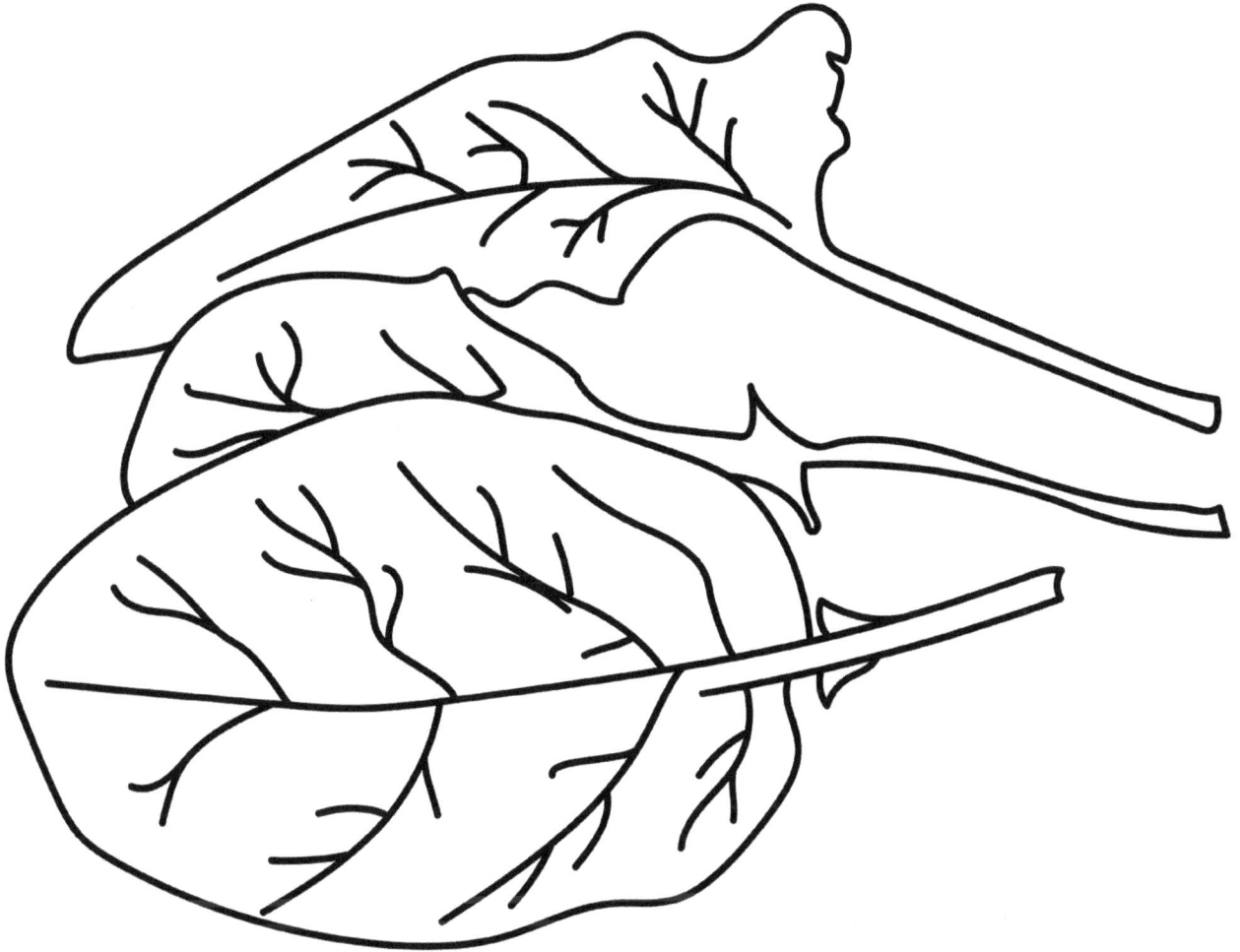

spinach

T t

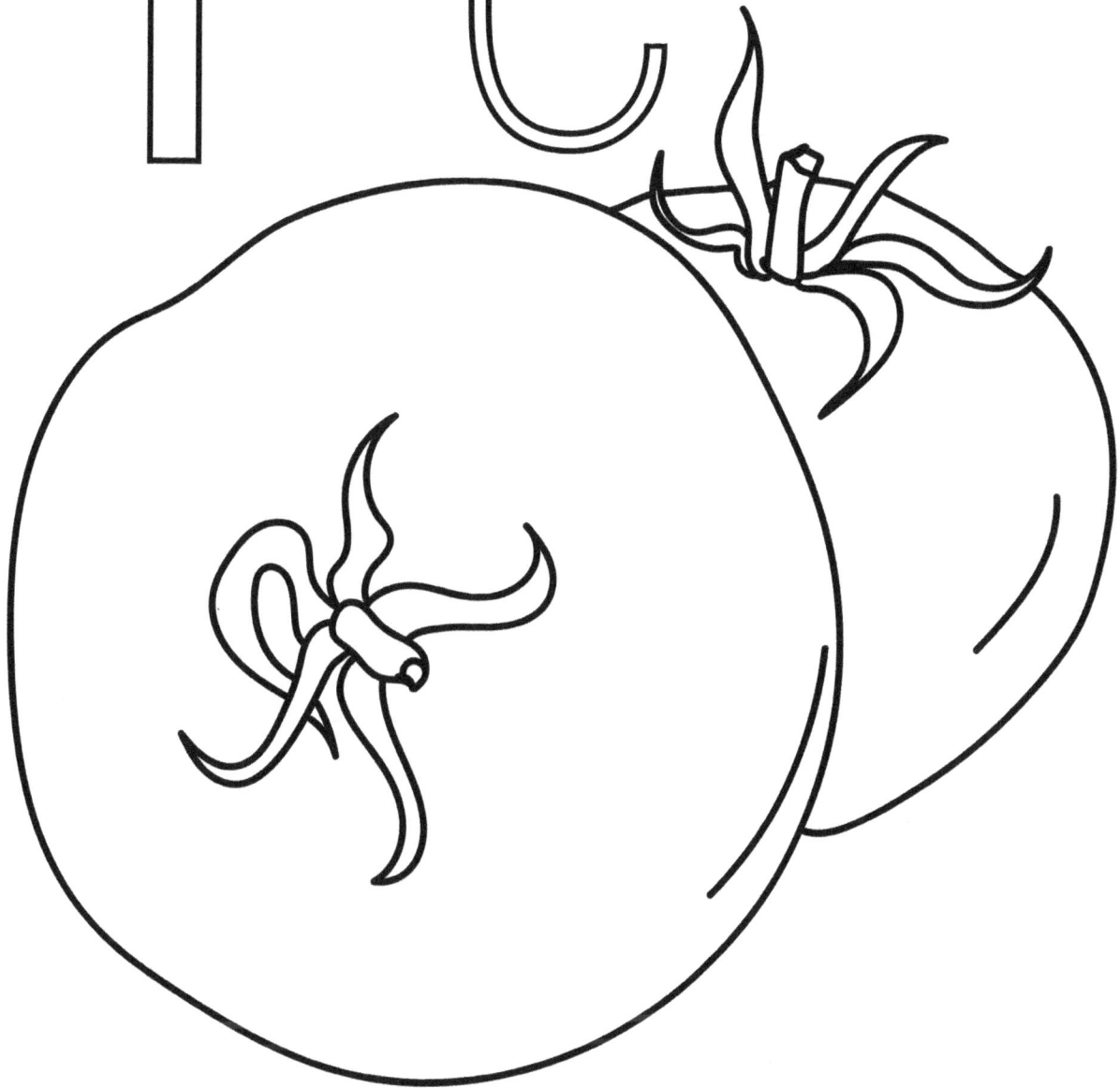

tomato

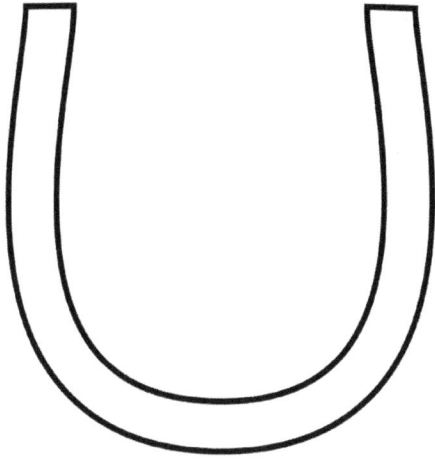

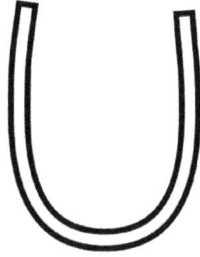

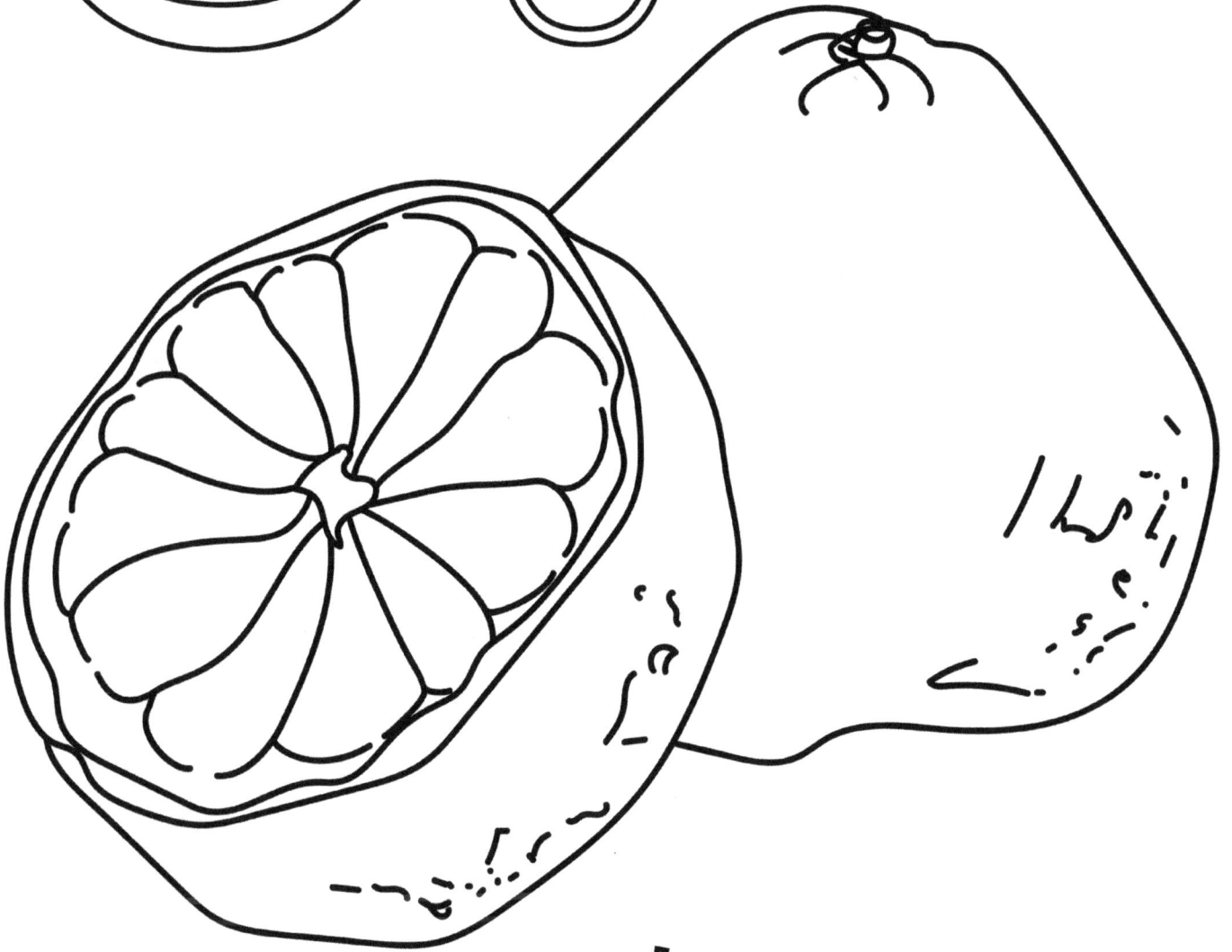

U u

ugli

Vv

vanilla

Ww

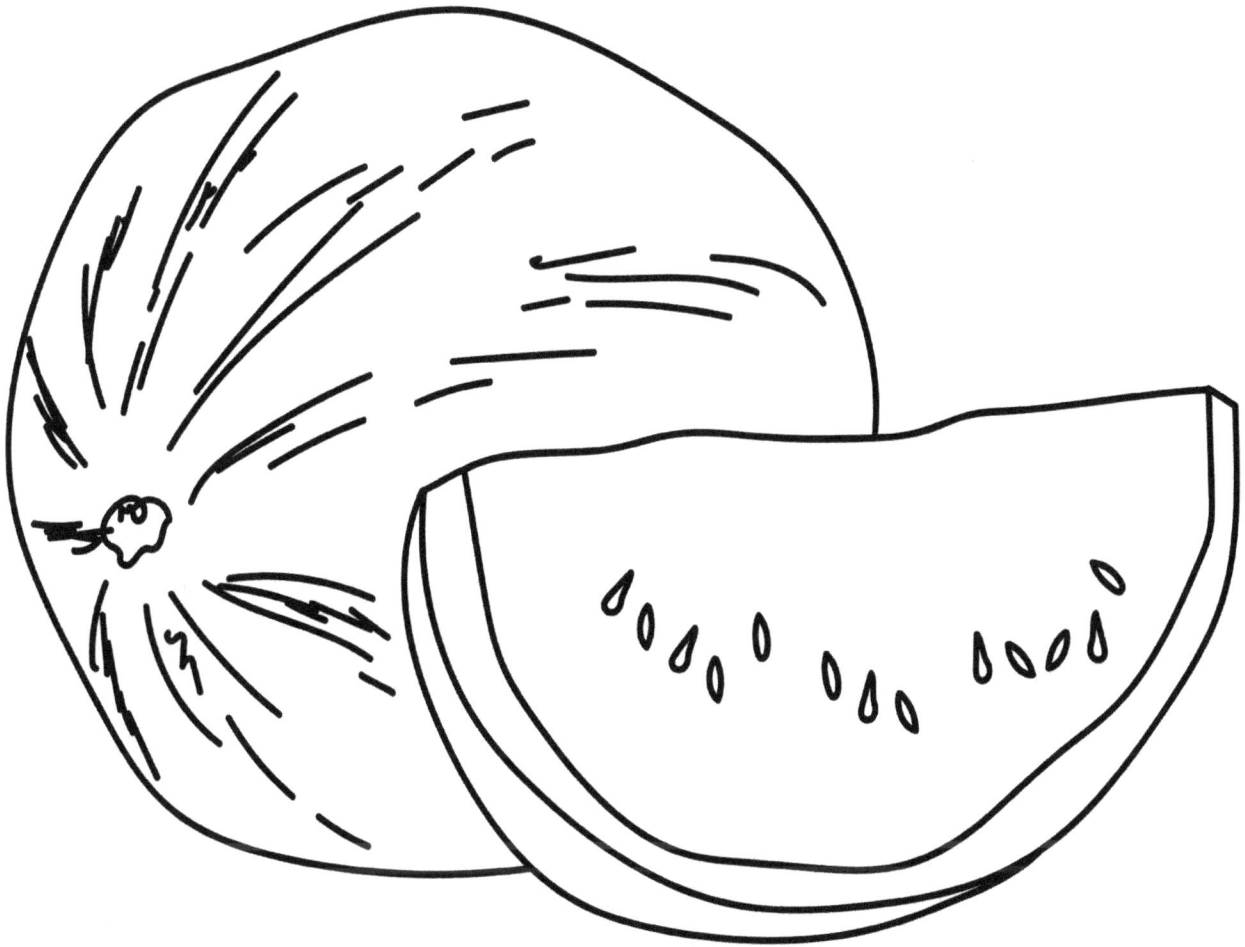

watermelon

X x

xigua

Y y

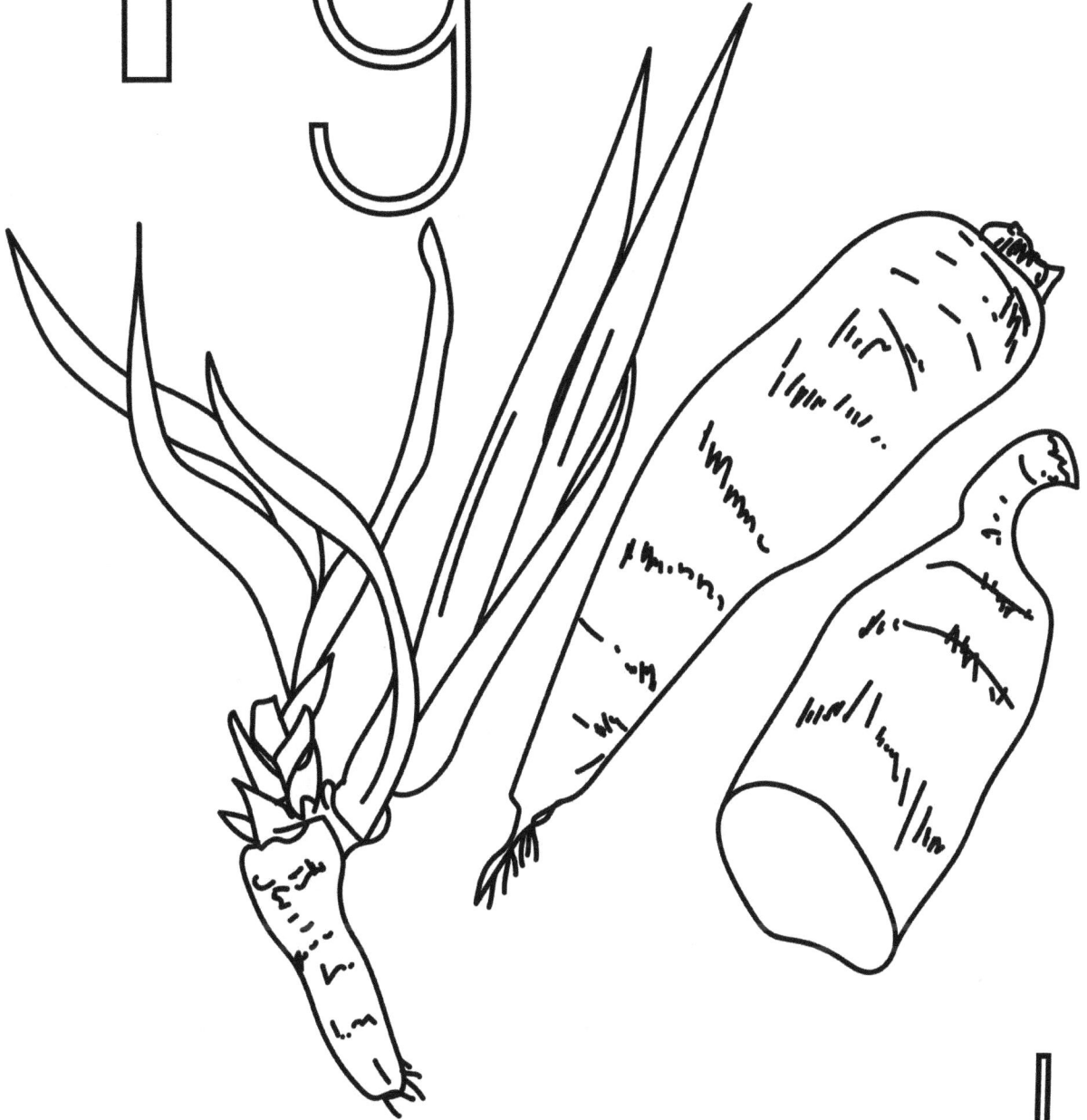

yucca root

Zz

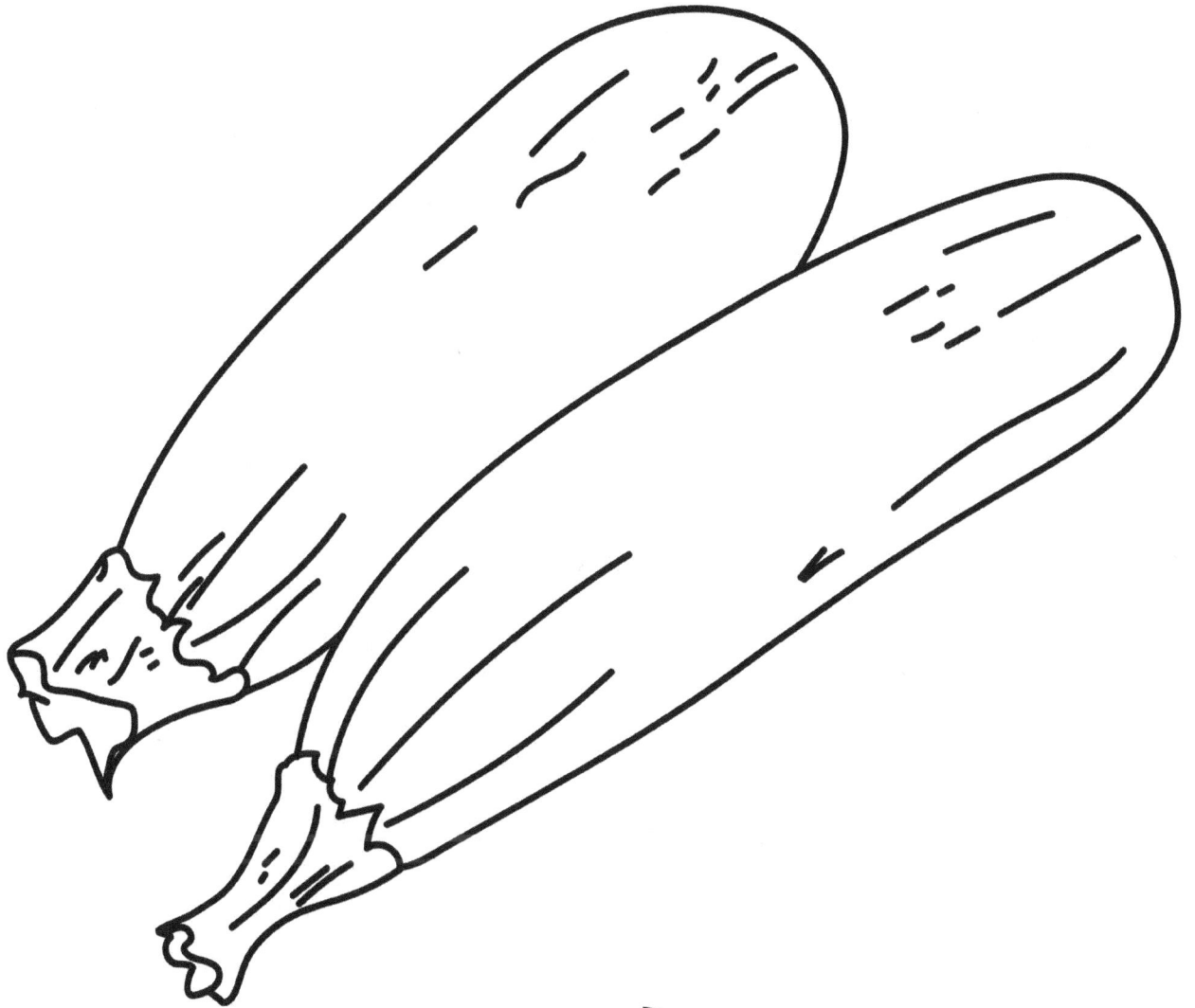

zucchini

www.ingramcontent.com/pod-product-compliance
Lightning Source LLC
Chambersburg PA
CBHW081230020426
42331CB00012B/3115